Isaiah
wants to
Read

by
Mykah Montgomery

To order additional copies of this book, contact:
Xlibris
1-888-795-4274
www.Xlibris.com
Orders@Xlibris.com

Isaiah Wants to Read is dedicated to you. You are precious in God's sight and in mine too.

Reading should not feel like a punishment or something you have to do. It can be fun and exciting when you find books that were made just for you. Begin your journey today; search for books that catch your eye. You will not know how awesome it is until you give it a try!

Always remember that you can do all things through Christ which strengthens you (Philippians 4:13).

With love,

Mykah Montgomery

www.mykahm.com

Isaiah Wants to Read

Mykah Montgomery

Isaiah Wants to Read is book #2 of the Mykah Montgomery OK2B Different series.

Book #1, ***The Little Girl Who Wanted a Tail,*** and its theme song Different, are about an African American girl who struggled with being different, but with the love and support of her family and belief that she can do all things, she became a confident child entrepreneur.

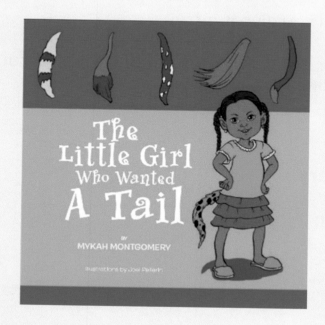

LISTEN:
"Different" http://mykahmontgomery.
bandcamp.com/track/different

WATCH:
"Different" music video http://www.youtube.
com/watch?v=irxtMd1TKeg

TALKBACK:
Facebook:
https://www.facebook.com/Ok2BDifferent
Twitter:
https://twitter.com/mykah72

AVAILABLE:
iTunes, The Little Girl Who Wanted A Tail - AMAZON.COM,
The Little Girl Who Wanted A Tail - BARNES & NOBLE.COM,
The Little Girl Who Wanted a Tail - Xlibris.com (Publisher),
and many online retailers - search Mykah Montgomery, *The
Little Girl Who Wanted a Tail* or Mylaan Imani "Different"

Isaiah King Matthews is a very special boy.

He loves books! Forget about toys.

Isaiah wants to read!

Is that a good thing for him to do?

If you said yes, then good for you.

Isaiah wants to read, and that's
exactly what he should do.

Why does Isaiah like to read?

I know other kids who don't feel the need.

Read a book, they'd say. Uh-uh, no way!

They'd rather use video games,
or go outside and play.

Sure, Isaiah likes video games, and he likes to
play, but reading is even more fun, he'd say.

When Isaiah was very little, his
mommy read to him before bed.

She held him in her arms and kissed him on his
head. "Isaiah, my love," his mommy said, "To be all
that God made you to be, you must read faithfully."

She went on to say, "In the image of God, you
are precious and wonderfully made, and will
do great and magnificent things someday."

Isaiah wants to read and his
mommy planted the seed.

Most of the stories his mommy read were short because she didn't have much time, but every story came to life in Isaiah's mind.

I mean, they really came to life every time.

Once he rode a lion down a street made of gold.

He was a king, he was fearless, and a sight to behold.

Another time he met the Lord Jesus Christ at his birth.

He was one of the three kings who brought him frankincense, gold, and myrrh.

He even started his own business like
The Little Girl Who Wanted a Tail.

Like her mommy said, a child of
God will always prevail.

What kind of business you ask?

A business teaching friends like
you that reading is a blast!

Isaiah wants to read, and that's
exactly what he should do.

It's fun, fun, fun for him and for you.

Do you want to read?

I think you do.

What's holding you back?

What's stopping you?

Some words Isaiah reads are hard to understand.

They are **BIG** words he found in
Vocabularyfunfunland.

Have you heard of *Vocabularyfunfunland*?

It's a place to learn, imagine, and grow—a
place that all kids should know.

In *Vocabularyfunfunland* you get smarter
all the time, and come back home with new
BIG words to use at the drop of a dime.

Vocabularyfunfunland doesn't let just anyone in.

You've got to be a reader and Isaiah's friend.

If you are just learning to read, that's great—YAHOO!

You are well on your way. Keep on trying,
and you'll be a strong reader someday!

If you've tried to read, and the
words just don't make sense.

Don't be tense.

Tell your mom, dad, teacher, or someone, and
they will get you help so reading will be fun.

Isaiah had trouble reading too, but he
never gave up, and neither should you.

Isaiah wants to read!

Is that a good thing for him to do?

If you said yes, then good for you.

Isaiah wants to read, and you should too!

It's fun, fun, fun, for him and for you.

The End

Vocabularyfunfunland Words

- Magnificent - extraordinarily fine; superb; noble; sublime

- Extraordinary – more than what is usual or ordinary

- Superb – excellent; very good

- Noble – high quality

- Sublime – outstanding; wonderful

- Prevail - to succeed/win

- Love – deep affection or emotion /warm positive feeling for another

- Isaiah - God is salvation

- Salvation - being saved from sin by the Lord Jesus Christ

- Sin - doing what we want to do when we want to do it rather than doing what God would have us do. Some examples of sin are bullying, lying, stealing, cheating, fighting, being mean to others.

- Practice the Greatest Commandment: Matthew 22:37–39 Jesus replied: Love the Lord your God with all your heart and with all your soul and with all your mind. This is the first and greatest commandment. [39] And the second is like it: Love your neighbor as yourself.

- Philippians 4:13 I can do all things through Christ[a] who strengthens me.

- Romans 10:9 - If you confess with your mouth the Lord Jesus and believe in your heart that God has raised Him from the dead, you will be saved.

Printed in the United States
By Bookmasters